The Drama of Mark

The Drama of Mark

MORNA D. HOOKER
AND
JOHN J. VINCENT

 EPWORTH

British Library Cataloguing in Publication data

A catalogue record for this book is available
from the British Library

978-0-7162-0664-4

First published in 2010
by Epworth Press
Methodist Church House
25 Marylebone Road
London NW1 5JR

Typeset by Regent Typesetting, London
Printed and bound in Great Britain by
CPI Bookmarque, Croydon CRO 4TD

Contents

Preface   vi

1 Mark as Drama   1
   MORNA D. HOOKER

2 Mark as Drama Today   35
   JOHN J. VINCENT

Preface

This little book had its origin in the weekend Annual Conference of the Student Christian Movement held in 2007.

On the Saturday morning, Morna Hooker, New Testament in hand, took the Conference through the Gospel of Mark. In the afternoon, John Vincent, with Morna Hooker's notes in hand, went through the same story as a contemporary twenty-first-century would-be disciple.

Fortunately the talks were taped. We have worked at them, and clarified them a bit.

We hope that the result will persuade others to hear and see the story, and then get their lives into it also.

MORNA D. HOOKER
Cambridge
JOHN J. VINCENT
Sheffield

Our special thanks go to Judith Simms for secretarial work at the Urban Theology Unit – whither royalties will go, with gratitude.

Bible translations

Translations of the Greek text are by each of the authors.

Mark as Drama

MORNA D. HOOKER

Context

Imagine, if you will, that you are sitting, packed closely together with others, in a room in a house somewhere in the ancient world towards the end of the first century. You have gathered together as a Christian community to worship, as you do every week. Normally when you gather you will sing some of the psalms from the Old Testament; you will listen to scriptures – Old Testament scriptures, that is, because the New Testament doesn't yet exist; you will hear someone speaking about Jesus – perhaps somebody who actually met him – and someone may try to explain what the death and resurrection of Jesus mean for them.

But today is a rather special day, because we have a special visitor – a wandering evangelist, who has brought a new book with him. He has not brought a box full of books, and he is not going to set up a stall in the market to sell them. He has, in fact, only one copy of his book, probably in the form of a scroll, so we are going to have to listen to it as it is read – and indeed that is probably the only way in which we ever have access to anything written, because most of us cannot read.

This is the reason, then, why so many of us have come today, and this is why we have all crowded into the house: we have gathered to listen as this new book is read. Our visitor stands up and begins to read: 'The beginning of the good news about Jesus, the Christ.'

Drama

Straight away, then, we know that the story we are going to hear is good news. But as we listen, we shall need to use a little more imagination, for this particular story will make us think, not that we are sitting cheek by jowl with our neighbour in a house, but that we are seated in a spacious amphitheatre somewhere in the ancient world; and this is because what we are going to hear is in the nature of a play reading – it is in effect a drama. So imagine yourselves now in the seats of an amphitheatre, looking down on the stage. The evangelist has come on to the stage and begun to read, and as you sit on your benches, watching the play unfold, you will probably be aware that on the horizon behind you there is a temple, which most playgoers would normally visit on their way to the theatre. Indeed, going to the theatre in the ancient world was quite often a religious experience. People went there not just to have a good time watching a play, but to worship in the temple, and the plays would remind them of the important role that the gods played in their lives, for the plays that people came to see were very often about the dealings of the gods with men and women. They might see a play about men and women living their lives and making mistakes, and quite often the story would be a terrible tragedy: partly that was because the gods were thought to be manipulating the strings behind the scenes, so the drama would tell a story about how the gods interact with men and women, using them for their own purposes.

Prologue (Mark 1.1–13)

But the story we are going to hear today is a rather different one. It is certainly a sacred story, but it is a story about a man called Jesus who lived and taught in Galilee, and as it unfolds we will realize that the God who lies behind this story is very different from the gods worshipped in the temple behind us. We begin – as all plays in ancient times did – with a kind of introduction, which will help us to understand the story. Already the first sentence tells us that it is about Jesus who is the Christ – that is, the Messiah. That is the main theme, but we need to know a little more about this Jesus, and we need to know a little about the plot. If you go to the theatre these days you usually have to pay about £2 for a programme, and as you look through its pages you will find, after all the advertisements and the life-stories of the actors, a little bit in the middle which gives you some understanding about what the action of the play is about; that is the important part, and it gives you what you need to know to understand the story. Two thousand years ago there were no programmes, but a prologue at the beginning of the play would provide everyone in the audience with the information they needed to understand the plot.

And that is what we are given, right at the very beginning of this drama. The story, we are told, is 'as it is written in the prophet Isaiah' – Isaiah, the prophet who foretold a time of liberation for his people, a time of forgiveness, a time when God would restore them and be known as their King once again, a time when they would be free from foreign domination. Our story begins, then, with a quotation from scripture, but the verse from Isaiah is introduced by a couple of lines from other Old Testament books, Malachi and Exodus:

> See, I send my messenger ahead of you;
> he will prepare your way. (Malachi 3.1)
> A voice crying in the wilderness:
> prepare the way of the Lord, make his path
> straight. (Isaiah 40.3)

The witness of John (Mark 1.4–8)

So who *is* this messenger? On to the stage marches the figure of John the Baptist. He appears in the wilderness – which means that the scripture is fulfilled – since he *proclaims* a baptism. He comes 'proclaiming' – so he must be the 'voice'. And what is this baptism that he proclaims? It is for 'the forgiveness of sins'. Forgiveness is on the horizon, and Mark reports that the whole of Judaea and everyone from Jerusalem flocked to hear him. We need to imagine the stage full of extras, all rushing to listen to John's message. The whole of Judaea? Everyone from Jerusalem? It sounds a bit of an exaggeration! But the point that is being made is that John has fulfilled his task – he has prepared the way; and we are all ready for what comes next – or rather for *who* comes next.

Then John the Baptist preaches a sermon. It is one of the shortest sermons on record, but like many sermons, it does have three points! Unlike many sermons, however, the message is very clear, because the points are all related. His message is this: 'somebody is coming who is stronger than I am; I am not worthy to stoop down and undo his sandals; I have baptized you with water, but he will baptize you with spirit.' These are three different ways of saying more or less the same thing – 'I am nothing, he is everything.' And who is this John the Baptist? Mark tells us that he is clothed in camel's hair and is eating locusts and wild honey, so we may well conclude that he is a bit of a crank. But if we know anything about the way in which the Old Testament prophets behaved, we will realize that what Mark is telling us is that he is a prophet, a man of the wilderness, and that we can take his word as authentic.

Jesus (Mark 1.9–13)

The crowds move into the background, and on to the stage marches another figure – Jesus. Presumably, then, this is the person about whom John has been talking, and immediately that assumption is confirmed. Jesus, Mark tells us, comes to John for baptism, and as he is baptized we hear a voice from heaven declare, 'You are my beloved Son'; at the same time we see heaven opened and the Holy Spirit descend on him. We are now certain that Jesus is the one about whom John has been talking, the one promised in the scriptures. And immediately after-wards, Mark tells us, this same Spirit drives Jesus out into the wilderness to be tempted by Satan, and there we see a battle taking place between Jesus and Satan. Mark gives us a very short account of the temptation, and we are not told what happened, simply that they met. We are not even told who won the battle – we are left to draw the conclusion for ourselves. And we are told that wild beasts were there, and that the angels waited on Jesus.

This, then, is the information that we are given at the very beginning of the story, and it is the equiva-lent of what we might be given in a theatre pro-gramme – and more! We have in fact been given a tremendous amount of theology in a very short space of time. We know that Jesus is the one prom-ised in the Old Testament, and that he is the ful-filment of scripture; we know that he has come to bring forgiveness of sins; we know that he is God's 'Messiah' or 'anointed', and that he is God's Son in whom God is well pleased; we know that the Spirit of God has descended upon him, and that he has confronted Satan in the wilderness. We need to remember all this if we are going to make sense of the rest of the story – which means that if you arrive late for the performance and come into the amphitheatre at this moment, you will be lost. You will not understand what is really going on, and you will in effect be in the position of the characters on the stage, for what you see taking place there is being played out by people who are unaware of any of these facts. Even John the Baptist doesn't seem to know who Jesus is, and certainly the crowds do not realize who he is. *Jesus* knows, and *we* know, but nobody else knows.

The characters in the story, then, are really in the position of latecomers to the theatre, who do not know what it is all about. Those opening scenes of the drama of Mark are pretty dramatic. They are also unusual. We are not going to hear voices from heaven every day of the week, and we are not going to see Satan appear again. What we have been given is special information to help us understand the rest of the story.

Jesus' authority (Mark 1.14–45)

And so we come to Act 1, Scene 1. If we are really to understand this story, then I suggest that we need to exercise our imaginations a little bit more. We began by imagining ourselves in a house somewhere in the ancient world, and then we imagined ourselves sitting in the amphitheatre. But now we need to imagine that we are on the stage, and that we are characters in the story, trying to make sense of what is going on. If we do that, we may have more sympathy for the Pharisees and the scribes than we normally do, because what is happening is so bewildering and unexpected that it is difficult to make sense of it. Jesus, we are told, appears in Galilee and proclaims, 'The Kingdom of God is at hand. The time is fulfilled.' And what are we to do? We are to 'repent and believe'. Our immediate reaction will be to say, 'Who does he think he is? Who gave him the authority to march into our town and our synagogue and proclaim this sort of thing?' There is no explanation, and since the characters in the story did not see the Spirit descend on Jesus or hear the voice from heaven, they are naturally in the dark.

The first thing that Jesus does in Galilee, Mark tells us, is to take a walk by the sea, where he meets a couple of fishermen, and says 'Follow me.' And what do they do? They down tools and follow. How surprising! He goes on a few yards and meets another couple of fishermen, and says, 'Follow me.' And they, too, down tools and follow. Quite extraordinary! What kind of a man is this, who has authority to issue commands in this way, so that people obey him? Why do they follow? Obviously he has enormous authority, but already in this opening scene in Mark's Gospel, we have been introduced to a theme which is going to be very important in this drama. The story concerns the good news about Jesus, yes, but it is also a story about discipleship.

Discipleship is a kind of sub-plot in the story, and it is one that is going to keep turning up right to the end. 'Follow me,' says Jesus, and then explains what following him involves. How do we respond to this figure, and to his command? Do we want to follow him or not? The challenge is already being thrown out to us in the audience, not just to those four fishermen.

Jesus comes into a synagogue and he preaches, and everyone is astounded. 'Wow!' they say, 'we have never heard anyone like this, and we have never seen anything like this.' In the synagogue, Jesus controls a man with an unclean spirit, and restores his sanity. And that is only the beginning of a series of stories, all of which hammer home the theme of Jesus' extraordinary authority. He preaches, he teaches, he heals. He even touches a leper and heals him! And then he heals someone who is paralytic, and he forgives his sins. And so the story continues and the evidence mounts up, and we are overwhelmed by the authority of Jesus.

Jesus challenges the religious authorities (Mark 2.1 – 3.6)

But woven into this theme of authority we see another theme, which is that Jesus is going to people who are on the fringes of society. He is not going to the religious authorities or to the biblical theologians, but to ordinary people and to people who are usually looked down on and excluded from society. A man with an unclean spirit? We don't want anything to do with him. But Jesus heals him. A leper? We must be very careful not to touch him, or we ourselves will be contaminated. But Jesus touches him. Someone who is known to be a notorious sinner? He does not belong to our society. But Jesus actually calls somebody who is a notorious sinner to be one of his disciples – he calls Levi to follow him, and soon after that he is seen at supper with a whole crowd of sinners. Oh dear! What sort of person is this? And what kind of authority is he exercising?

Then Jesus starts doing things which, according to the religious authorities, are infringements of the law. According to what is said in the Old

Testament, one must not work on the Sabbath, but Jesus is healing on the Sabbath; surely he should not be doing that? But Jesus challenges the authorities, saying, 'Look, who is *really* obeying God? Is it you, who stick to the strict letter of the law, or is it me? For what I am doing is to *fulfil* the law by bringing salvation. So which of us is *really* doing the will of God?'

Jesus, then, is pointing beyond the strict letter of the law to the real *purpose* of the law – in other words, he is coming up against the fundamentalists in the ancient world. This story begins to have a modern ring to it!

Discipleship (Mark 3.7–30)

In chapter 3, Mark pauses for breath as it were, and reminds us of the story so far, in case we have got lost. This is one of the arts of the storyteller, because of course we are not really taking part in the original events, nor are we even in an amphitheatre watching the story being enacted on the stage. No, we are in that crowded room, listening to our visitor tell a story. And because the room is almost certainly getting a bit hot, and because one or two of us may even be nodding off, every now and then our storyteller throws in a summary – the kind of thing you get at the beginning of an instalment in a television serial – reminding us of the story so far. From time to time, then, Mark reminds us of what the story is about: of how Jesus came proclaiming good news, and called men and women to follow him, and of how he taught them and healed them, and challenged them.

But now, in chapter 3, he tells us how Jesus chose twelve disciples to be with him and learn from him: we are back once again to this theme of discipleship. There is now a small band of people who are committed to following Jesus – but then, in contrast to this, we learn that some people are rejecting him. Among his opponents, two groups in particular are singled out. The first is a group of religious bigwigs – scribes who have come from Jerusalem, the equivalent of the Archbishop of Canterbury's envoys, who come to inspect what is happening and make sure things are being done properly, but who conclude that they are not. They sit listening to Jesus disapprovingly, asking one another, 'How is this man managing to heal? He must be using the power of Satan.' Jesus responds by saying that they do not know the difference between good and evil, and that they are confusing Satan with the Holy Spirit, since they are attributing to Satan the work of the Spirit. Now, if you think back for a moment and remember that opening scene where we saw the Spirit of God descend on Jesus, and then immediately afterwards saw him battling with Satan in the wilderness, we realize that Mark gave us there the clue that enables us to understand what is happening, and that it is indeed the work of the Spirit that is being seen in Jesus. So these religious authorities are calling white black; it is an awful warning to anyone who claims to be a religious teacher!

Rejection (Mark 3.21 – 6.6)

But there is another group of people who are opposed to Jesus, and that, surprisingly, consists of members of his own family, who say, 'Oh, he must be out of his mind to behave like this.' They come and stand outside the house where Jesus is teaching, because they do not want to have anything to do with the group of disciples round Jesus. So we have this great division taking place, a division which Jesus then spells out in the parable of the sower. This is a very carefully crafted story about how the seed fared. The seed fell on various kinds of ground, and because much of it was for one reason or another unsuitable, the seed that fell there failed. But some seed fell on good ground and produced a crop – some of it good, some excellent. Although the story is full of detail, the basic contrast is between seed which does not grow and seed which does. It is a parable about what is happening in Jesus' own ministry – some of his hearers respond, some do not. By telling it, Jesus confronts the crowd with a challenge: how are *you* going to respond? 'If you have ears to hear, hear,' he says. 'If you have eyes to see, see.' The trouble is that most people do not use their eyes, and do not use their ears, so they are deaf and blind to the truth.

As we continue listening to the story Mark tells, and watching scene after scene on the stage, we learn more and more about Jesus and what he did. We listen as he tells a whole series of stories which leave his audience astonished. We watch scenes in which he heals the sick, or performs acts of power which leave people completely overwhelmed. We see him feeding the people, and then stilling a storm, and each scene confronts us with the question, 'Who is this, that he can do these things? What kind of power are we seeing here?' Some of the people present at the time dismiss what they see; Jesus comes to his own city, to Nazareth, and they say, 'Ah, we know this person, he is the local carpenter, he cannot be anything special,' and so they forget about him. But others give a very different answer: the themes of rejection and discipleship go side by side.

It is at this stage in the story that we are told that Jesus sent out his disciples to extend his work. Disciples were not called simply in order to sit there listening, they had to share Jesus' mission, and so they were sent out to preach and to heal.

The death of John (Mark 6.7–29)

So far in the narrative the spotlight has been on Jesus – he has been in every single scene that has taken place – but at this point he withdraws, and we have a kind of intermission. John the Baptist reappears. At the very beginning of the Gospel, we learned that the Baptist had been put in prison, and now Mark tells us what happened to him there. He tells the story very well, but it is an unusual one, about dancing and adultery, and about how John the Baptist's head ended up on a platter. It is a somewhat graphic and dramatic tale, and we may well wonder why Mark is devoting so much space to this story. Unlike everything else in Mark's account, it does not seem to be about Jesus at all. At the end of the story John is beheaded, his disciples come and take his body away and bury it. And that is the end of John.

So why has Mark included this story about John? Well, if you think back to the very opening scene, you will remember that John was the messenger, the forerunner of Jesus, who announced his coming by proclaiming the message he had been given. Now he seems to be acting as the forerunner in another way, because those of us who know the *end* of Mark's Gospel will remember that in the closing scenes we are told how Jesus died, and how some of his disciples (though not the twelve!) buried his body in a tomb. Except, of course, that that is not the end of the story about Jesus. Nevertheless, we have a parallel between what happens to John and what happens to Jesus, and it seems as though at this point Mark is saying, 'Look, the end of this story about Jesus is inevitable. If they rejected the forerunner, they will reject the one who follows.'

The turning point (Mark 6.30–8.38)

After this we have more stories, all involving what we may perhaps call the 'Wow! factor'. We are told about another feeding, and about another occasion on which Jesus crossed the sea – this time in a truly remarkable way; then we have two stories about healings – one telling how a deaf man was suddenly able to hear, the other describing how a blind man gradually recovered his sight, at first dimly, then fully – and we are reminded of the parable of the sower, and of Jesus' words about people who are blind and deaf because they fail to use their ears and their eyes. Now two people have gained their faculties – they can see, and they can hear. But what of the disciples? I have said that this is a story about discipleship as well as a story about Jesus, and now the two themes are brought together. Jesus asks his disciples, 'Who am I?' And Peter says, 'You are the Christ, the anointed.'

In his lectures on Greek tragedy, Aristotle said that in the middle of a tragedy there always comes a turning point, a scene in which there is recognition, when the scales fall from the characters' eyes. In the story of Oedipus, for example, there is a scene in which he realizes that the man he has killed is in fact his own father, and that the woman he has slept with is his own mother: suddenly the terrible nature of the situation he is in is revealed. At this point in the drama, the characters in the story begin to understand who everyone is, and to realize the terrible nature of the tragedy in which they are involved.

We have such a moment at Caesarea Philippi. For the first time, the disciples realize who Jesus is – something *we* have known from the beginning of the story. And because we have known this, we have been wondering how long it would be before the disciples understood who Jesus was, and why they were so dim that they were unable to put two and two together! Finally the penny has dropped, but with it comes the revelation that the end of the story is going to be a tragic one, for Jesus immediately goes on to say, 'The Son of Man must suffer and be put to death, and be raised from the dead.' Except, of course, that the disciples are not prepared to listen; their reaction is to say, 'No, no, no, don't talk such nonsense!' They are not ready to see the truth after all. Like the man whose eyes were opened and who began to see, though only through a blur, the disciples are still able to see only half the truth, and so remain uncomprehending.

The implications of discipleship (Mark 9.1 – 10.32)

The next few scenes in Mark concentrate on the meaning of discipleship, but interwoven into the story is this theme of Jesus' identity. Almost immediately after Peter has blurted out his belief that Jesus is the Messiah – God's anointed one – we are taken up the Mount of Transfiguration, where the disciples see Jesus, together with Elijah and Moses, in glory, and hear a voice from heaven telling them that he is God's Son. We, of course, have known this from the very beginning, but now these three disciples are let into the secret. The scene on the mountain reminds us of the story in the Old Testament about Moses hearing God speak to him on Sinai. Now the disciples are urged to listen to the words of Jesus – and to obey him.

Once again the revelation of Jesus' identity is followed immediately by warnings about what is to come. The conversation on the way down from the mountain is about Jesus' death and resurrection. The link between John the Baptist and Jesus is spelled out. John the Baptist (referred to here as 'Elijah') has been put to death, so what is in store for Jesus himself? The link between Jesus and his disciples is also stressed, since from this point on, the implications of following this Messiah are underlined. 'The Son of man must suffer and die,' he said in chapter 8, and then went on to say, 'If anyone among you wants to be my disciple, you must take up your cross and follow me.' When we remember what crucifixion meant in the ancient world, we realize that this is anything but an encouraging invitation. We treat these words all too glibly, since they do not mean anything to us any more. But crucifixion was the most barbaric form of execution ever devised; this is hardly the way to recruit followers!

In the next couple of chapters, Jesus spells out what it means to be his disciple. Every time he talks about his own suffering and death, he tells the disciples that they must be prepared to follow the same path. In chapter 9, Jesus repeats his warning that 'the Son of man must suffer and die'. This time, the disciples start arguing about which of them is the greatest; clearly they have forgotten that following Jesus does not involve being considered 'great'. Jesus turns their ideas upside down. At the end of chapter 10, we find a very similar scene: first, Jesus says that 'The Son of man must suffer and die', and immediately afterwards, two of the disciples come to him and ask, 'Can we share your glory when you sit on your throne?' 'Can you share my baptism?' he asks. 'Can you share my cup?' Sharing his glory means being prepared to share his fate; the true sign of greatness is to save others. Discipleship is no longer looking a very attractive option, and we may well find ourselves wondering whether we want to stay with the group of disciples surrounding Jesus, or whether, instead, we are going to join forces with the family of Jesus, who remain 'outside' the circle of his followers, and the religious authorities, who are opposed to him. Do we *really* want to follow this sort of Messiah?

And so we approach Jerusalem. As Jesus leaves Jericho, another blind man appeals to him for help; Jesus heals him, and the man follows Jesus on the road. Where is that road leading them? It is taking them to Jerusalem, and to all that is going to happen there. This once blind man is apparently willing to follow Jesus as a disciple, for Mark tells us that he follows him 'on the road' – the road that leads to Jerusalem. But does he realize that this means that he must be prepared to suffer and die with Jesus?

The King comes to Jerusalem (Mark 11.1 – 13.37)

Jesus enters Jerusalem, and now the cards are laid on the table. He enters as a king. His disciples commandeer a donkey, and Jesus rides into Jerusalem. Why a donkey? 'Oh,' we think, 'that must be because a donkey is a nice peaceful animal.' But that is to miss the point! Jesus and his disciples enter Jerusalem with other pilgrims – but pilgrims did not ride into the city; they came in humility, on foot. But here is Jesus *riding* into Jerusalem, and those who know the scriptures well will remember the story in 1 Kings telling how, when David lay dying, his son Solomon was brought into Jerusalem on his father's mule and crowned as king. And now Jesus, the King of Israel, comes to Jerusalem riding on a donkey, in order to be crowned.

Jesus comes into the temple, and rejects the shallow worship that he sees taking place there. The people are in effect *failing* to worship God, and have reduced the temple to a market place. Jesus is challenged by the religious authorities about his own authority, but instead of giving them a direct answer, he poses a question: like all good teachers, he wants others to work out the truth for themselves. He sets them a conundrum, and says, in effect, 'Think about it.' 'What about John the Baptist?' he asks. 'Did his authority come from God, or did it come from men?' Here is a tricky question for them to answer! If they answer 'God', then he will surely ask them why they did not listen to him. If, on the other hand, they say 'Men', they know that the people will not like that, since they think that John was a prophet. The priests and elders are stumped, for they do not know how to answer. But Jesus' challenge is far more than a clever trick question. What he is doing is to point his opponents back to the work of John the Baptist, and ask them to think about what both he and John have been doing. If John prepared the way for the salvation which Jesus is bringing, that means that John's authority is linked with that of Jesus. In other words, if they can find the right answer to the question Jesus is posing, they will find the answer to their own, and they will realize that Jesus' authority – like John's – comes from God.

In chapter 12, we have another parable, and once

again it is a parable about harvest. In chapter 4 we had a parable about sowing seed, and about the different kinds of harvest the seed produced. This time we have a parable about a vineyard. The owner of the vineyard demands his due return: he wants his share of the crop. But the vineyard tenants hang on to it: they are not going to hand the harvest over. Once again, then, the parable is about the failure to produce what is expected. In the first parable, the seed failed to bear fruit – or a lot of it did – and in this the tenants are clinging to the harvest, because they do not want to give up the grapes. So what is going to happen? They are going to lose what they have. 'From him that has shall be taken away even what he has.' In other words, this is a parable about judgement. And that is the overall theme of these final chapters of Mark. Jesus is pronouncing judgement on people for failing to give God what is God's right, and failing to worship him aright. Remarkably, however, one person is singled out for praise. It is a woman, a widow, who throws everything she has into the temple treasury.

Faithful women (Mark 12.41–44; 14.1–9)

One of the most interesting things about Mark's Gospel – have you noticed? – is how well the women do. The disciples are continually misunderstanding, and the authorities keep making mistakes, but the women in Mark's Gospel are commended right from the very beginning. Peter's mother-in-law serves Jesus – she is doing the right thing, as we learn later on in the Gospel; a desperately ill woman touches Jesus in the crowd, trusting that she will be healed; a foreign woman pesters him, convinced that he can and will cure her daughter. All these women are commended for their faith. And now, as Jesus leaves the temple, he praises this woman, who has given everything she has to God, for her generosity.

As the final act in the drama begins, we find another woman spending a fortune on Jesus – and he commends *her*, too. It is typical of Mark that he describes how ordinary people respond to Jesus, while the religious big-wigs fail to do so. Jesus helps people who do not count, people on the margins of society – foreigners, lepers, 'sinners', women – and they respond. Now a woman comes to Jesus at supper, and anoints his head with precious ointment, and Jesus commends her, saying that her action is a sign of his forthcoming burial. An ominous note! But perhaps it is a sign of something else as well. Who was it that normally poured out ointment on someone's head? It was the high priest when he anointed the king. Is it a bit far-fetched, we may wonder, to suggest that Mark sees this scene as the anointing of Jesus as King? How could a *woman* do this? Well, as we have seen, women do remarkable things in Mark's Gospel! And as we shall discover in the chapters that follow, Jesus' death is linked in closely with the idea of his kingship. It would seem that in anointing him for burial, the woman is also anointing him as King.

Trial and testing (Mark 14.10–72)

At the beginning of the Passion narrative, therefore, Jesus, who has ridden into Jerusalem on a donkey as King, is anointed – as King. We now move through the terrible events of the last hours of Jesus' life: the Last Supper, Jesus' words about his coming death, and Gethsemane, where Jesus agonizes over whether he must indeed drink this cup, where he is shown as obedient to God, and where the disciples all fall asleep – a sure sign that they are going to fail in the coming test.

Then we have the betrayal by Judas, followed by dramatic scenes of Jesus' so-called 'trial' before the high priest. At this point we have to envisage the stage being split into two – we have one scene taking place at balcony level, and another being played out down below, and they are taking place simultaneously. Mark is inviting us to see the parallel between the two. Upstairs, in the grand hall of the high priest, Jesus is being arraigned on a charge of blasphemy: 'Are you the Messiah, the Son of the Blessed one?' For the first time in this story Jesus acknowledges openly that he is both Messiah and Son of God: fearlessly he answers, 'I am.' This is an extraordinarily powerful scene.

Meanwhile, down below in the courtyard, we see Peter. Everyone else has run away, so let us at least give Peter credit for having crept into the high priest's house. He has come into the courtyard and is warming himself by the fire. And then a maid sees him and says: 'Ooh, you are one of his disciples'; straight away Peter denies knowing Jesus. It is not as though he is being asked to confess Jesus as the Christ – rather he denies even knowing him, and he does it not once but three times over. Remember how the disciples fell asleep three times in the garden, when Jesus had urged them to stay awake and pray that they did not succumb to temptation? It is hardly surprising, then, if Peter denies Jesus three times; nevertheless, the contrast between the two scenes that take place simultaneously – Jesus confessing his identity, Peter denying him – is dramatic.

The King is enthroned (Mark 15.1–47)

Jesus is now taken before Pilate, on an accusation that he has made himself 'King of the Jews'. If you read this part of the story carefully, you will see how often Mark emphasizes Jesus' kingship. He is referred to as the King of the Jews and the King of Israel, and the charge against him is that of being the King of the Jews. Mark is telling us, not about the execution of a malefactor, but about the crucifixion – the enthronement – of a King. Jesus is crowned with a crown of thorns and given a purple cloak; he is mocked as King, and is finally enthroned as King on the cross, where he is mocked by bystanders. And that, they must have thought, would be the end of the story – except that as Jesus dies, his executioner says, 'Surely this was the Son of God'; and so for the first time in the Gospel, we find in a human mouth the acknowledgement that Jesus is God's Son, a truth that you and I have been privileged to know from the very beginning of the story. And who is it who makes this proclamation? Not the high priest, for though he had enquired, 'Are you the Son of God?', he had certainly done so mockingly. The only person actually to speak these words believingly is the centurion who is Jesus' executioner. Mark's picture is extraordinary: the first person to acknowledge Jesus as 'Son of God' is not a Jew, but a Roman, an outsider!

What kind of a story is this? What kind of a coronation is this? What kind of a Messiah? What kind of King? At the very end of the story, disciples bury Jesus' body – but they are not the twelve, since they have all let him down. Judas has betrayed him, Peter has denied him, and the other ten have deserted him. It is someone called Joseph of Arimathea who finds a resting place for the body and puts it in a tomb, and the only people to witness what is done are the women, standing by the cross and watching the burial, still faithful, still doing the right thing.

Epilogue (Mark 16.1–8)

So we come to the final scene. It is a bit unexpected – a kind of epilogue. If this were truly a tragedy following the rules of Aristotle, then the burial of Jesus should be the final scene, since the story normally ends with the death of the central figure. But not this story. Three days later, Mark tells us, the women set out for the tomb, in order to anoint the body. 'Silly women,' we think – you cannot anoint a body three days after someone has died, for, in the Palestinian climate, that is much too late! Their task is impossible – and indeed unnecessary, since the woman at Bethany anointed Jesus' body *before* his death!

As for their conversation, that is even more absurd. As they walk towards the tomb, they ask one another, 'Who is going to move the stone for us when we get there?' You would think that they would have thought about that before they started out, and taken a strong man with them! But of course, all the strong men have run away. And when they arrive at the tomb, they discover that there is no need to move the stone, since it has already been rolled away; and no need to anoint the body, since it is not there. The point of their 'foolish' question is, of course, to remind us how big the stone is, and to make us realize what an enormous event has taken place – the stone has been moved and the body has gone. Instead of the dead body they expect, all they find is a young man sitting in the tomb saying calmly, 'He is not here, he has risen, and he has gone to Galilee. Go and tell his disciples that if they want to see him they must follow him to Galilee.' It is hardly surprising if the women take to their heels and flee!

I have said that the women do very well in Mark's Gospel, but at this point I am afraid that even they let us down. They are scared stiff – and who can blame them? – and so they flee. At some point, however, they must have told others what they had seen and heard, otherwise you and I would never have heard the story. *Somebody* passed on the good news, and presumably the terrified women eventually did so. But what an extraordinary ending to the drama this is! We have come to the end of the story, and what are we given? All we are offered is a scene in which a message is sent to the disciples telling them that if they wish to see Jesus, they must go to Galilee. And then everyone flees from the stage. Does Mark's ending leave you feeling let down? Why does he not describe a wonderful scene in which Jesus appears to his disciples? That is what the other evangelists all do. Has the end of Mark's story been lost, as people long supposed? Did mice nibble the end of that first scroll, and could nobody remember how the story should end? Did Mark perhaps die before he could finish his book? Or is this perhaps one of those stories that has a 'suspended ending', leaving its readers – you and me – to complete it for ourselves?

The challenge

If it is, then this is the point where it is necessary to have a little audience participation, for this is not a drama where you are expected simply to sit and watch; rather it is a drama which should have been challenging you from the very beginning. Mark's whole story is in fact an invitation to see Jesus from his point of view – the viewpoint of an evangelist, a bearer of good news, who is convinced that Jesus is the Christ and the Son of God. The challenge with which he presents us at the end of the story is to demand that we, too, respond to the angel's message. If we want to see Jesus for ourselves, then we, too, must set out to see him, like the disciples. It is no good just sitting here in our seats, relying on the evidence of other people who say, 'Yes, he is indeed alive again.' It is no good relying on stories to the effect that he was seen and touched, no good looking for what we call tangible evidence – *concrete* evidence – that he has been raised from the dead. The only way of knowing that Jesus has been raised from the dead is experiencing him and meeting him for ourselves. And to do that, we must be prepared to follow where he has gone.

And so the final scene at the very end of this drama is not a triumphant one in which Jesus returns to his disciples, but simply a young man standing on the stage pointing in the direction of Galilee and saying, 'If you want to see him you must follow after him.' Those words echo something we heard earlier in the story; they remind us of Jesus' call to follow him – and that, we remember, involved taking up the cross and following in his footsteps. Do we really want to be disciples of *this* sort of a Messiah – a Messiah who was crucified? But apparently, if we want to see the risen Christ, then that is what we must do. Mark's drama has turned into a kind of evangelistic rally, and one by one we, the audience, have to decide whether to sit still in our seats or to get up and go off to Galilee, trusting that there we shall see Jesus.

What Mark has done, then, in presenting us with the story of Jesus, is to challenge us by saying, 'Do you want to be disciples of this Jesus?' If you do, then you must not only listen to his story, you must join in. This is not the kind of story that can be read and then closed up in a book and put aside, to be consulted only occasionally, like a recipe book or a car manual, or a book of rules providing guidance when something goes wrong. It is a story which invites us to take part, by committing ourselves to following Jesus. Mark is inviting us to share in his faith, and his book is a witness to the living Christ who is calling us to follow him. 'If you want to see him, you must follow after him.' It is only those who are prepared to commit themselves to discipleship who will meet the risen Lord.

Suggestions for further reading

Ernest Best, *Following Jesus: Discipleship in the Gospel of Mark*, JSNT Supplement, Sheffield: Sheffield Academic Press, 1981.

Ernest Best, *Mark the Gospel as Story*, Edinburgh: T. & T. Clark, 1984.

Morna D. Hooker, *The Message of Mark*, London: Epworth, 1983.

—— *A Commentary on the Gospel According to St Mark*, London: A. & C. Black, 1991.

—— *Beginnings: Keys that Open the Gospels*, London: SCM, 1997.

—— *Endings: Invitations to Discipleship*, London: SCM, 2003.

R. H. Lightfoot, *The Gospel Message of St Mark*, Oxford: Oxford University Press, 1962.

David Rhoads, Joanna Dewey and Donald Michie, *Mark as Story*, Minneapolis: Fortress Press, 1999.

W. B. Telford, *The Theology of the Gospel of Mark*, Cambridge: Cambridge University Press, 1999.

Mark as Drama Today

JOHN J. VINCENT

The challenge

This part of our book starts where the first left off with the conclusions:

> 'If you want to see him you must follow after him.'
> 'Get up and go off to Galilee, trusting that there we shall see Jesus.'
> 'It is a story which invites us to take part, by committing ourselves to following Jesus.'

So this part is an account of the drama of Mark's Gospel as it has been followed by a few people in contemporary Britain. And that means starting all over again, at the beginning, and then following it stage by stage in our own life today – or at least, in the lives of one group of would-be disciples.

Context

Imagine, if you will, that you are sitting in a room with ten or a dozen others, somewhere in contemporary Britain at the beginning of the twenty-first century. You have gathered together in what we call our 'Gathering'. Like the first followers, we meet not in a synagogue or a church, but in each other's homes.

In fact, in our contemporary Burngreave Ashram (in Sheffield) of the Ashram Community, we meet fortnightly in each other's homes at 7 p.m. We bring food, which we share together, sitting as far as possible around the large kitchen or dining-room table. Then we move to the sitting-room, and share concerns and plans for our common life, followed by a member leading us in one of our Community Worship Liturgies, or in open prayer and sharing of personal and political concerns. Then, at about 8.30, we take it in turns to introduce a current subject, campaign or relevant topic, or a Bible study, or part of the Ashram *Journey* course. This takes us to 9.30 or 9.45, when we give each other lifts back to our own homes or to one of the Ashram Community houses, where we live.

Drama

Meeting after meeting, we get out the Gospel and put ourselves back again with those first disciples, listening to the drama of Jesus and his mission on earth.

Actually, our meetings in each others' homes are very like the meetings in which Mark's drama of Jesus was first read. But now the drama is not simply 'out there'. The drama is 'in here'. The first hearers of the Markan story were on the edges of their seats in the amphitheatre or in each other's tenement living-rooms in the first century because they believed that the story of Jesus was still going on in their streets. And they were not mere spectators but actual participants, because they were called to do what he did.

So we today, as we sit watching TV or travel to work or read the newspaper, are hearing and reading the context for the walk of Jesus in our time. And we, sitting together in each other's homes, or sharing in our community's life and projects, are involved in a contemporary walk with him, following in his footsteps, walking in his way.

We're asked, 'Come right down here, out of your seats. Come down and join us at the platform,' as Billy Graham used to say. Come down and see how far his journey could inform and enlighten your journey, and how far you could journey 'with him, and what in practice that journey might mean', as our *Journey* course has it.

The call of Christianity as a continuing drama, as we develop it in the *Journey* course, and in what follows here, is a perhaps more modern – or even postmodern – way of using Gospel stories. In the past, the emphasis was more on intentionality, motivation and spirituality. The classic Ignatian Exercises indeed led to practice, but through an elaborate interior discipline. Here, we go for imaginative identification with Gospel action more directly. And we do it with the whole life of Jesus, and not mainly with the Passion, as in Thomas à Kempis's *Imitation of Christ*. And we see the key in corporate and community engagement in the drama, rather than personal, or primarily personal. Our 'imitation' is not of disposition, but of practice and method, and we 'risk ourselves' not just solo, but with sisters and brothers alongside us – as Jesus did.

So where will his drama lead us?

Prologue (Mark 1.1–13)

Mark tells us how Jesus got on to this stage of history by going to John the Baptist, who was his 'Prologue'. Mark's readers must each have had their own 'Prologue', a person or event or community that brought the drama of Jesus on to the stage of their lives.

It's a question for each of us. How do I get to be here in this little community of friends to whom Mark's messenger brings this story? On any normal reading of things, it is certainly extraordinary that a twenty-first-century person would feel attracted into this first-century story.

It makes you reflect on who or what functions as your 'Prologue'. For myself, I first became drawn into this story by being befriended by a generous, gentle and imaginative group of his disciples who gathered together in a church near to where I lived as a youngster. They were an open, liberal and caring group who organized all the activities of a fairly prosperous suburban church, with classes of all kinds – a guild, a dramatic society, a youth club, a junior club, a choir, and societies for male and female members. They also invited groups into their own homes for fellowship gatherings or for social evenings and occasional parties.

Within this warm and supportive environment, I first encountered Jesus and his stories. I was invited to teach a class of small children, so learned to tell the story simply. I was asked to help with the morning Sunday School, so obtained a few basics –

a New Testament, and a book of Christian writings to be used in brief addresses or teaching. Especially, I recall frequently using a book called *Thus Spake Jesus* by Aubrey Rees, and an anthology of religious writings, plus a few special books like Khalil Gibran's *The Prophet*. This was the tiny armoury of self-assembled pieces which I had at 18 as I started two years of National Service.

You could say that I landed in this Jesus gospel by accident. But I chose to stay there. Both things were probably true of Mark's readers. They are probably true for you too.

The only conclusion is: treasure your Prologue!

The witness of John (Mark 1.4–8)

Jesus' story, says Mark, began with John the Baptist. For Mark, John represents the prophets from the past – who now only reappear in Moses and Elijah at the Transfiguration, to leave in their place 'Jesus only'. Now, listen to him!

John the Baptist says that the coming one is going to baptize us with Spirit. That means that we are all part of the new development. One of the key tasks of the one who has come, who has himself just received the Spirit, is to make sure that everyone else gets the same Spirit – and does what

Spirit-inspired people do. What is that? Wait and see, says Mark.

Jesus

Morna Hooker tells us that the characters in the Gospel story are like latecomers to the theatre who have missed the opening scenes, and have to get into the scenes without the 'backdrop' of the first ones. That is very like most of us today. We don't have the background of the Old Testament, so it's not really significant to us whether Jesus fulfils this or that. And we don't get voices from heaven.

So what we have to do is to be open to the impact of each of the scenes that follow, and just imagine ourselves into the drama, purely on the base of the story. Here, the disciples are so crucial for us, because that is what they had to do. Where he goes, they go. The troubles he gets into, they get into. His lifestyle of giving up everything for the sake of the good news of God's realm on earth, they have to adopt. The cup and cross he has to take, they have to take.

So we see Jesus through the eyes of his disciples. They were there, most of the time. Tradition says that Mark wrote down Peter's recollections. Whether or not that is the case, it's a disciple's Jesus that we are given.

And more: if we want to put ourselves with this Jesus, we learn how to do it alongside these disciples, learning how to do it, and how not to do it, with them.

To use Morna Hooker's image, we are now also 'characters in the story, trying to make sense of what is going on', because we have to learn from Jesus, and from the disciples who are with him.

Jesus' authority

The first thing we have to learn as disciples today is that Jesus has come with a stupendous claim that there is now a completely different situation present on earth. His authority is the self-possessed 'power' that energizes everything he does. At the start, he announces his mission. We need to see it as it is in the Greek text, and not as nearly all our translations rewrite it. It goes like this: Jesus came into Galilee announcing the good news from God:

> The realm of God is now present here on earth.
> So change yourselves completely,
> And trust yourselves to this good news. (Mark
> 1.14–15)

Whenever Mark says that Jesus or disciples preached or taught, this is what they were preaching and teaching. Mark has no other 'content' to the message. For him, this is enough.

The next verse takes Jesus to beside the lake, calling disciples. The implication is clear. There is now a completely new situation for human beings on earth. In this special person, the full force and ethos of the Eternal is present in time, on this planet, in this community. What is needed as a consequence is not 'believing in it' but 'trusting ourselves to it'. The appropriate immediate response is not discussion or study, prayer or spirituality, but preparedness to leave our nets or parents behind, and get up and go after this person – which is exactly what the two pairs of first disciples do, and what Levi the tax collector in the next chapter will do.

The peremptory call to discipleship as Mark describes it has produced endless improvements. The later Gospel of John has a more rational story, of one person telling another, 'Come and see who we have found. It's the Christ!' Even Luke sets the call to discipleship addressed to fishermen who have just witnessed a miraculous catch of fish. But Mark's story preserves the mystery and the arbitrariness of the call. There is no real justification or even explanation.

In August 2008, 20 members of the Ashram Community spent a week at Iona Abbey, living with the community there. One morning, we studied 'The Implications of Discipleship' in Mark's Gospel. We divided into five groups to look at five passages concerning discipleship: The Call (1.14–20), The Common Mission (2.13–17), The Community (3.13–19), The Common Disciplines (6.8–11), and The Personal Consequences (10.28–31). We asked ourselves four questions about discipleship in each passage:

1 What are the *characteristics* of discipleship here?
2 What *process* is taking place in discipleship?
3 What *degrees* of discipleship are evident?
4 What exactly is *shared* here?

The first group, studying the Call passages, discovered these elements:

1 *Characteristics*: You're called to it. You don't volunteer. How much consent is there?
2 *Process*: 'Follow me' is totally open-ended. You could end up anywhere.
3 *Degrees*: For these first five, it's a literal 'leaving behind' of everything else. They become wandering campaigners, like Jesus.
4 *What is shared*: A promise – 'I will make you'.

Jesus challenges the religious authorities (Mark 2.1 — 3.6)

Morna Hooker dramatically summarizes the effects of Jesus' mission under this heading. What Jesus does in acting out God's present realm on earth is good news for some and bad news for others. In fact, division and controversy are vital elements that go with every aspect of the mission of Jesus. They are decisive elements in any Jesus-coherent mission practice that we might get into, in my experience. So this section is rather long!

As I developed ideas or principles for urban mission, I discovered that Mark has a fairly consistent strategy for his mission stories. We may take the story of Levi as typical. Four elements are present.

THE MARKAN MISSION PATTERN

Place

The scene is set. The context is specified. The location in which the action takes place is named.

The dramatic location for the Levi story is summarily indicated. It is the toll-station, the taxation office, the local base for the Roman taxation system. In the time of Jesus, Roman local taxation charges were extracted from the people in occupied territories by a variety of means. The most obvious, and the one which affected ordinary people most, was the system of placing taxes on goods as they were being transported from one place to another – typically from country farms or vineyards into the cities or markets.

Person

The key person in the little drama, as in many other Gospel encounters, is named.

The villain who has to assess what Roman tax is due, and receive the sum due, is the collector of taxes. He has a name – Levi. He might be known to some of Mark's readers. Or he might be known to you or to me.

This is the person Jesus invites to be a follower. Jesus so far has got the two brothers, Simon and Andrew, and the (we think) two teenagers, James and John. They are probably faithful members of the Galilean community. But Levi is not. He is a quisling. He is a betrayer of Judaism to the enemy. He makes a living out of extracting money from his fellow countrymen, and paying it to the Romans. And he himself has to earn a living out of the surcharge which he levies on the goods passing through, which he adds to the fixed Roman levies which he has to pass on to the authorities. This is the person Jesus wants!

Practice

Next, in this place and with this person, Jesus does something decisive.

One of the things that Jesus' followers obviously do is to open their houses to him and his disciples. This is what had happened with Simon Peter's house. So now that Levi is a follower, Jesus and his entourage have to come round for a meal. Disciple-ship is immediately a practice – sharing a celebrat-ory meal.

Mark adds that other tax officials, and law-breakers, were present. 'Sinners', as our transla-tions put it, is not correct. The people concerned were those who by their genealogy or physical state or profession, or those who in the pursuit of their profession, were ritually unclean, and thus could not carry out the Old Testament laws and the scribal regulations. In those terms, they were non-compliants with the laws and rituals of Israel. So far as Israel was concerned, they were disobedient to the law, which meant that they were, in the terms of the law, violators of the law. And all violators of the law were the non-righteous – that is, 'sinners' in the eyes of the law.

Jesus says a very striking thing about these people. They are not evil-doers. They are sick people, and as such do not need the legal exclusion customs of a hard-line righteousness, but rather the generous, healing out-going of a physician. Yes, says Jesus, I know they are outside the law, but they are not outside God's community. I have come to throw out the bounds of God's community, to break down the 'hedge' that the scribal regulations have made around the law. I have come, Jesus says, to draw a wider circle, which includes them inside it.

Purpose

The fourth stage is a statement or saying summarizing why the story is important.

Sharing a meal with someone in that society is a demonstration of total acceptance and mutuality. The shared meal is a sign and symbol of this new, wider circle of those who are within God's present divine community here on earth.

'He eats with tax officials and people outside the law,' the Pharisees complain. 'Indeed I do,' replies Jesus. Moreover, the distinctive and effectual sign of this new family of God on earth is a celebration banquet, a wedding feast. And for this new marriage between divinity and humanity, the marriage feast is necessary and proper. Fasting disciples are no use – feasting disciples are necessary and proper. We feast to celebrate that God's home is now with and within humanity. And disciples, taking their cue from Jesus, are his friends, his 'best man', his mates. 'This is no time for fasting,' says Jesus.

Mark follows this comment of Jesus by an odd saying: 2.20 rather misses the point of his own theology. Instead of giving voice to the evident continuing identification of the early Christian communities with the continuing privilege and obligation to reflect Jesus' banquet-welcome to all sorts and conditions of people, Mark has Jesus reflecting on the short time of the Passion – a time when Jesus will be taken from them. But that three days was followed by Jesus going before his disciples, back into Galilee, so that they would continue to encounter him there, continue the banquet of his presence.

This was the purpose of the practice – to celebrate God's realm on earth. The earliest Christian communities continued this 'commensality' practice of Jesus, his 'banquets', his 'marriage feast'. They continued to share open, inclusive meals together 'with glad hearts and common spirit', as it says in Acts

2, to carry on the celebration and keep the purpose clear.

So far as discipleship is concerned, the second Ashram/Iona group concluded on the Common Mission passage of 2.13–17:

1 *Characteristics*: Four levels of followers emerge: the inner core of now six co-practitioners, the 'many' people brought in by Jesus' practice, the crowd around, and the critics observing.
2 *Process*: The disciples are thoroughly into the Jesus practice, repeat it, get questioned about it, even instigate it (with rubbing the corn).
3 *Degrees*: All the 'many' do not become fellow-journeying followers.
4 *What is shared*: Home, hospitality, food, reputation, alignment with dodgy people.

Discipleship (Mark 3.7–10)

The disciples in Jesus' day were head and shoulders into Jesus' practice. That is clear. But how do we as disciples today get in on the act? By following the Markan pattern of Jesus' mission in some mission of our own. I give an example from my own life.

THE MARKAN PATTERN IN PRACTICE

Place

When in 2000 the Ashram Community bought the rambling, largely disused premises of 80–86 Spital Hill, Sheffield, the building was in the centre of an inner-city, multi-ethnic, multi-faith street. There were drug dealers and prostitute pimps on the corner outside the shop. Cadillacs drew up, and a protection racket kept local traders in awe. I remember asking, as I put up the shutters one evening, 'What on earth has brought us here?'

What on earth in fact had brought us here was this memory of Jesus going among the tax collectors. It had said to us: 'Find the place nearest to people in need.' That's why we landed here!

Person

But the druggies and the pimps and their ladies? Daily we picked up needles on the pavement. What good could we possibly be to people like this?

We opened the corner shop as a sort of market and café, and waited to see who would come in. We must have a low threshold, we said.

Slowly, people came in. Not, in fact, the druggies. But the typical people of any deprived inner city – people with mental problems or depression, young single mums with their toddlers, failed white middle-class people who could live cheaply in the inner city where their parents would not visit them. These must be people we had come for!

Then we found homeless asylum-seekers sleeping on the streets, and let some of them come in and sleep in our cellar. A year later, we had first-floor accommodation available, so we fixed it up, and four failed asylum-seekers joined our small residential community.

Practice

The Gospel-style practice is the action of Gospel-style missioners ministering to the place and to the people.

The place needs a project which has a low threshold – which makes it easy for all sorts of people to come in. It needs to be accessible, both in its entrance and in its style within. We developed easy and cheap offers – tea or coffee and cake for 75p, soup and bread for 50p (the prices in 2004).

We encouraged particular groups of people to come in and have social meetings over tea or coffee. This has brought in the local clergy team, area health workers, library staffs and campaigning groups. We have several individuals, community workers, who are regulars. A group of mental health workers and clients currently run a 'Knitter-Natter' two hours. The latter takes place in the shop next to the shop/café, with an internal access door. There, too, other groups meet – a group who campaign for specific asylum-seekers to be allowed to stay, and a group helping disabled asylum-seekers.

Purpose

As in Mark's pattern, the purpose or significance of a story often comes at the end – in Mark's case, frequently in response to some question or criticism from religious authorities.

Early on, we called Burngreave Ashram 'A sign of the Incarnation, and a place where Kingdom of God things might happen'. Later, we began to realize how useful it was to have a non-Christian word like 'Ashram' in our title, so we described ourselves: 'As an Ashram, a place for personal and group spirituality, open to people or all religions and none. As a Christian Ashram, with its base in the radical Christian tradition, which expresses itself in the Gathering.' We also have a multi-faith chapel and library, and see it as a symbol of our character, alongside our neighbours – 27 faith groups of every kind in

Burngreave. So we say: 'An inner-city Christian Ashram welcoming all faiths and spiritualities.'

Rejection (Mark 3.21, 31—6.6)

So far as Burngreave Ashram is concerned, the churches in general ignore what we do. The surviving members of the Sheffield Inner City Ecumenical Mission (SICEM) still support us, with quarterly United Services in our place and in their places. But SICEM no longer has denominational support – and consequently has no money for staff, and little money for projects.

Rejection? Well, by and large, our family and relatives find it all very odd, even though they support our hospitality to needy people and to asylum-seekers. In fact, as other churches get smaller in numbers, they are becoming more like us, so the smaller churches empathize with us.

The parables in Mark 4 are, as Morna Hooker says, about 'this great division', in which relatives say 'He's out of his mind', and one or two people have 'ears to hear' and 'eyes to see'. The parables teach you that there is absolutely nothing whatsoever that you can do with people who cannot hear or see what is really going on. But that's the majority – most people, says Morna.

What a gospel person is doing is imitating Jesus. Jesus was only a carpenter. What could he do? Well, Jesus is saying that the truly significant thing is the leper who gets healed, the tax collector who gets changed, the man with the withered hand who gets it cured. These tiny incidents are pieces of history and reality that sink into the ground, and apparently die. But they don't die, they bring forth 30, 60 or 100 more, or grow secretly till harvest, or become a great tree that people can shelter in. It might look like a tiny light, but you put it on a lamp stand, and everything will get lit up by this tiny light (4.21).

And that tiny light is appearing outside the holy nation. The storm is stilled at the end of chapter 4 to get the Jesus movement over to the pagan territory of Gerasa; and soon, in chapter 7, Jesus is going to be inveigled into healing a Gentile woman's sick child. What has been rejected in Jesus' native religious community is bringing forth fruit completely outside it. It makes us reflect much at Burngreave that Jesus' ministry takes him more and more into his multi-faith environment.

That's what Kingdom projects are like.

So thank you very much, 'this little light of mine, I'm gonna let it shine', 'You in your small corner, and I in mine'.

This is the real revolution. This is the famous stone that turneth all to gold! These tiny implantations of seeds are the way the world gets changed. So Jesus, according to Mark – and we, following at a distance!

The death of John (Mark 6.7–29)

We're in the inner city. For five years we've had yearly fatal shootings on our streets, local people caught up in drug feuds.

But everyone has some friends. Disciples come and take the body, and lay it in a tomb. Families grieve. Neighbours share. Religious leaders say prayers. Police and community leaders meet. Some good comes. The young man shot in 2007, Jonathan Matondo, at one time was going to be a preacher when he grew up. Someone else will have to do it now.

The mystery and agony of death on our streets is a sign nevertheless of life in the midst of death. I find myself moved by this recurring life and Passion narrative – for me, nowhere better done for contemporary urban Britain than in Jon McGregor's *If Nobody Speaks of Remarkable Things*. Which reminds us never to not speak!

The turning point (Mark 6.30 — 8.38)

It's all got very public – 5,000 fed, 4,000 fed, storms stilled, the twelve spreading the mission, crowds following, deaf hearing, blind seeing. Bits of the promised realm of God on earth are now coming to reality all around. Yes, it's got to be God's anointed one doing all this! ('Christ' or 'Messiah' means 'anointed one'.)

But what kind of anointed one?

It's the new humanity, says Jesus. 'Son of Man' means simply 'Man' – human being. What is going on is what a truly human person would be doing. And we are to be part of it. It's a corporate Son of Man now. He's not alone. We're part of him.

We're part of him as the New Humanity. But he's still the first New Human, and we are only disciples. So how has our discipleship been going along?

The implications of discipleship (Mark 9.1 — 10.32)

Earlier, I started to tell you about two of our Ashram groups on Iona, working at the implications of discipleship for us today.

The third group worked with the Community passage, 3.13–19. Here, Jesus describes the purpose of his company of twelve: 'To be with him as his companions (so the New English Bible), to be sent out to proclaim (that is, proclaim God's realm now present on earth), and to carry out healings and exorcisms.'

The group concluded:

1 *Characteristics*: Jesus chooses 'those whom he wants' – a crazy mix of irreconcilable men from widely differing backgrounds.
2 *Process*: He selects people for the next stage, and names them as individuals.
3 *Degrees*: Other followers continue to follow, but are not in this 'Mission Band'.
4 *What is shared*: Common disciples, common life, food, accommodation, common ethos, common task, being tribal heads in God's new community on earth.

All of these were tested out when, three chapters later, the twelve were sent out on the Mission. The fourth group, which studied the Common Disciplines, as in 6.8–11, concluded that further implications of discipleship were:

1 *Characteristics*: Work authorized by Jesus, a minimalist lifestyle, reliance on others' hospitality.

2 *Process*: Jesus' work is now extended through pairs of fellow missioners.

3 *Degrees*: Unexpected hosts are also part of the movement, but don't become itinerants.

4 *What is shared*: Similar conditions, equality of call, empowerment.

As Morna Hooker says, in Mark 9 and 10, 'Jesus spells out what it means to be his disciple'. Much of these chapters show disciples walking in a completely different direction – objecting to Jesus' destiny of crucifixion, refusing to see that they must follow him, to share his baptism and his cup, and even trying to secure honours for themselves, or be considered great. Indeed, it's a healed blind man who 'Follows him in the Way' – ironically never said of the disciples, whose job it is!

All of this leads many readers today to look at contemporary disciples, and particularly contemporary congregations and denominations, and observe that they exhibit some very similar traits!

But Mark has Jesus in fact confirming these disciples.

We got our fifth Ashram/Iona group to get into the Personal Consequences passage of 10.28–31. Jesus has just been explaining how hard it is for rich people to enter God's realm, and the disciples say

to each other, 'Who then can be saved?' Then Peter says: 'We've left everything to follow you', and
Jesus replies: 'Anyone who has left house, brothers,
sisters, mother, father, children or lands for my sake
and the good news's sake, gets a hundredfold of
each of them now in this present time.'

The group concluded:

1 *Characteristics*: A negative view of what most of
   us spend all our time on!
2 *Process*: When do we get the hundredfold? It's
   hyperbole, but about proportional compensations.
3 *Degrees*: You get more if you give up more. Is this
   not true in Christian community?
4 *What is shared*: Mutual support, common priva-
   tions, each other's families and homes, persecu-
   tions, 'eternal life'.

Contemporary disciples today have as much trouble
in all this as their first-century predecessors. But this
'Losing life' is what Jesus calls 'Gaining Life' (8.35).

Is it all too much? Dietrich Bonhoeffer, in *The
Cost of Discipleship*, says that it's costly because it
costs your life, but it is *grace* because it's Jesus who
you're called to follow. I often say, when people say
that it's all too much: 'Go for as much as you can
of it.' 'Go for what's going for you.' Don't say, 'We

can't have all things in common.' Say what things you *can* have in common.

The King comes to Jerusalem (Mark 11.1–13.37)

This entry of Jesus into the city has always been a real 'call' for me. I've often reflected: is the Church, or our project, or even we disciples, the ass on which the Lord now rides into the city? I called my first book on urban discipleship *Into the City*, after that verse of the hymn, 'Tell me the stories of Jesus':

Into the city I'd follow
The children's band
Waving a branch of a palm tree
High in my hand.
One of his heralds,
Yes, I would sing
Loudest hosannas:
Jesus is King!

From the perspective of the inner city, it is always a real question, how we get Jesus and Jesus-style enterprises into the city itself, which is the centre of power and privilege. Are we relevant at the top table? In 2006–7 I was Lord Mayor's Chaplain for one of our local councillors, Jackie Drayton. We both wanted to take Burngreave into the Council Chamber – but we only partly succeeded.

Morna Hooker says that the parable in chapter 12 about the tenants keeping the harvest to themselves, which ends up with it all being taken from them, is to illustrate 'From him that has shall be taken away even what he has.' Is that about people in power?

In these days of globalization, credit markets, banking failures and economic collapse, we have to say: 'We Christians keep propping up the city. But does it really prop us up – us and, more importantly, what we stand for? Or is the city always going to reject Jesus and his so-called good news?'

And will it always be the case that those crying 'Hosanna' will only be the crowd he has brought with him, 'running ahead and following behind' (11.9)?

Faithful women (Mark 12.41–44; 14.1–9)

'How well the women do' in Mark has led to several very striking books and articles by women scholars recently.

As a man, I find it odd that women still get included in lists of 'people on the margins of society – foreigners, lepers, "sinners", women'. Women have always made up half the human race, after all!

So far as Christian communities and churches are concerned, we have always been two-thirds or three-quarters women. In the working-class street-corner chapel, the women might have elected their quiet, submissive husbands as stewards, but the real power was always in the Sisterhood, the Women's Bright Hour, or the Young Wives' Club – or in the kitchen rather than the vestry.

What was radical in Christianity was that women anoint the King. Happily, in all but hierarchical, dictatorial church organizations, they still do. Or become kings themselves.

Trial and testing (Mark 14.10–72)

But now I get to be less and less part of the story. I have never 'resisted unto blood' (Hebrews 12.4). I've had a few experiences of being arraigned before the Methodist Conference, which I would not wish on anyone. But they (presumably!) repented, and a decade later elected me their President.

I hope I've never been a betrayer. I've had the experience of being betrayed, a few times. It certainly is no fun. And if my trust in another was too naïve, that makes it no better. Mark does not go for pathos. It's Luke (22.48) who has Jesus say: 'Betrayest thou the Son of Man with a kiss?'

'Don't bring us to the test' is in the modern translation of the Lord's Prayer. God wouldn't do it. But other people will, like the maid with Peter. Except that, like the rest, we'd have already forsaken him and fled.

The King is enthroned (Mark 15.1–47)

Well, but our man, our hero, our champion, our leader, is still King. Whose King? Pilate wants him landed on God's ancient people. Priests and Pharisees want the regicide landed on Pilate and Rome.

Christian sensitivity has always avoided the political debate about who's to blame for what happened in first-century Jerusalem. Does it matter which of them was mainly to blame? If I'm a follower, the question is, 'Where am I?' So the hymn 'O Dear Heart Jesus' (*Herzliebster Jesu*):

> Who was the guilty? Who brought this upon
> Thee?
> Alas, my treason, Jesu, hath undone Thee.
> 'Twas I, Lord Jesus, I it was denied Thee.
> I crucified Thee.

'I don't know how to love him,' says the musical *Godspell* lyric. I don't know what to do here. To linger in these unspeakable scenes, gloating over the Passion of Christ, helps nothing. Crucifixions were numerous in Jesus' day, and their equivalents are in the world today. And we seem unable to call a halt to it all.

At least, I helped start CND in 1957, and I support the Campaign Against the Arms Trade. But what do I do to build a world economy not dependent upon nuclear 'defence' and war? We in Britain still sell arms around the world.

Epilogue (Mark 16.1–8)

If I want to see Jesus, he is not here. I cannot anoint his dead body. I do not need to roll away the stone from the tomb. He is not there.

Where is he? He has risen. He has gone to Galilee. Tell disciples everywhere that if they want to see him, they must go back to Galilee, follow him back to Galilee.

I believe that. Mark has no resurrection appearances but this promise – Go back to Galilee, and you'll see him there. What does it mean? Were there actual appearances in Galilee? We do not know, at least not from Mark.

More and more of us conclude that what Mark was saying was that the whole mystery and obedience of the Gospel is a perpetual going back to

Galilee. OK, we followed his project through this time round, and it all ended in tragedy. But he's gone beyond it now. He's gone back to the beginning again. We've got to start all over again as well – back to Galilee, and new places, people, practice, purpose and new projects.

The Challenge

So if we want to be involved in this drama, and be his disciples and serve his new community of God on earth today, we will doubtless also get it wrong. But there is no point in staying at the cross or the tomb. He is not there. The cross is empty. The tomb is empty. The real presence of Jesus is now where it was then and always has been – in embodying God's realm on earth, in calling a community to extend it, in bringing in anyone who will come to share in it, in breaking down the bonds that keep people from it, in celebrating its presence in our practice, and in pointing to its sustaining power in our church community life.

If you've got this far, you need to go back to the first part of our book to check that you've got it right, and then to the first page of this second part, because that's where we repeat the challenges with which the first part ends.

Or perhaps you have got to decide – OK, I'll give it a go. Let's see how far I can get with it. Let's see where it leads me in the world today and tomorrow. Let's see what place and people and practice and purpose it opens up, what project it lands us in. The project is the key.

And let's discover for ourselves what the characteristics and process of the stories, and the degrees of discipleship, and the ways of sharing within the stories, mean for our discipleship today, in terms of lifestyle, vocation, economics and community. The way we do the project is the key.

And if that is all still strange or even impossible for us, let's find other disciples and communities that might help us.

Suggestions for further reading

The method of interpreting the gospel stories by showing what they lead to in contemporary action is called 'Practice Interpretation'. Three books edited by John Vincent contain examples of this by a variety of scholars and practitioners:

Mark: Gospel of Action: Personal and Community Responses, London: SPCK, 2006.

Stilling the Storm: Contemporary Responses to Mark 4.35 – 5.1, forthcoming.

Acts in Practice: Practice Interpretation of the Acts of the Apostles, forthcoming.

The method of Practice Interpretation itself is described in:
Outworkings: Gospel Practice and Interpretation, Sheffield: Urban Theology Unit, 2005.

Material on the contextual background of the Gospels is in John Rogerson and John Vincent:
The City in Biblical Perspective, London: Equinox Press, 2009.

Further material on 'Living with the Gospel' in practice is contained in other books by John Vincent:
Hope from the City, Peterborough: Epworth Press, 2000.
Discipleship, Pocket Radicals 1, Sheffield: Ashram Press, 2007.

A 12-part 'Explorations into Discipleship', following stages of Jesus' life and ministry and experimenting with their implications today, is in the course, *Journey*. Volumes are:
Journey: Explorations into Discipleship, Sheffield: Ashram Press, 2003.
Journey Resource Book, Sheffield: Ashram Press, 2005.

Other books referred to

Dietrich Bonhoeffer, *The Cost of Discipleship*, London: SCM Press, 1948, rev. 1959.

Khalil Gibran, *The Prophet*, London: Heinemann, 1947.

Jon McGregor, *If Nobody Speaks of Remarkable Things*, London: Bloomsbury Press, 2002.

J. Aubrey Rees, *Thus Spake Jesus*, London: Epworth Press, 1943.

Lightning Source UK Ltd.
Milton Keynes UK
21 February 2011
167907UK00007B/62/P